Contents

CB081851

Macmillan Education
4 Crinan Street
London N1 9XW
A division of Macmillan Education Limited

Companies and representatives throughout the world

Ferris Wheel 2 Activity Book ISBN 978-1-380-01870-0

Original design by Clare Webber
Page make-up by emc design ltd
Illustrated by Jose Ignacio Gómez (Nacho Gómez) pp5–7, 9, 15–16, 18–19, 22(a,c,f,h), 23(a,f), 25–27, 35–36, 43t, 45–49, 53t, 55–56, 65–66, 75–77, 79, 80t, 83 (main character artwork illustrations). Other illustrations by Animation Group Sp. z o.o. pp3–4, 8, 13b, 17, 22(b,d,e,g,i), 23(b–e), 28, 33, 37–39, 42, 43b, 48b, 53b, 57–58, 59, 63, 67–68, 73b, 78–79, 82–83 (in the style of Nacho Gómez); pp.29, 49c, 50–52, 54, 69, 94–96 (own style); Arpad Olbey (Beehive Illustration) pp10–14, 20–21, 24, 30–34, 40–41, 44, 60–62, 64, 70–74, 80b, 81, 84–93.
Cover design by emc design ltd
Cover illustration by Jose Ignacio Gómez (Nacho Gómez).

Authors' acknowledgements
I would like to thank everyone at Macmillan Education in the UK, Spain and Mexico who has contributed to the development and production of these materials. I would also like to thank all the teachers who have taken time to read and pilot the materials, and given invaluable feedback at every stage of writing the course. Special thanks as ever go to my husband, Alan, for his encouragement and support, and to our son and daughter, Jamie and Hannah, from whose early childhood days I learnt so much.

The publishers would like to thank Alex Tamulis, São Paulo, Brazil; Ayşegül Sezer, İNO Schools, Turkey; Daniela Araujo Pielli, Alt Idiomas, São Bernardo Do Campo, Brazil; Daniela Pugliese, Milton's College, Buenos Aires, Argentina; Esra Ezici, Turkey; Fernanda Domeniconi Nery Amorim, São Paulo, Brazil; Gabriela Iocolari, English Schoolhouse, Buenos Aires, Argentina; Gulbin Cin, Bahcesehir College, Turkey; Mariana Pastorino, Em Pi Instituto de Inglês, Santa Fe, Argentina; Mariné Ortiz, Warrington, Buenos Aires, Argentina; Paola Daniela Tuninetti, Academia Argüello, Córdoba, Argentina; Silvana Paola Accardo, Escuela Cooperativa Mundo Nuevo Instituto Casa de Jesús, Buenos Aires, Argentina

Printed and bound in Brazil.
2025
52

Point and say the names. Trace and color the Ferris Wheel. Say the colors.
Language: Mommy, Daddy, Mimi, Dylan; Ferris Wheel; blue, green, orange, pink, red, yellow

Find and color the toys. Point and say. Ask and say.
Language: ball, car, doll, teddy, train, scooter; blue, green, orange, pink, red, yellow; Where's the (ball)? Here's the (ball)! It's (blue).

Classroom

Fun with paint!

Vocabulary

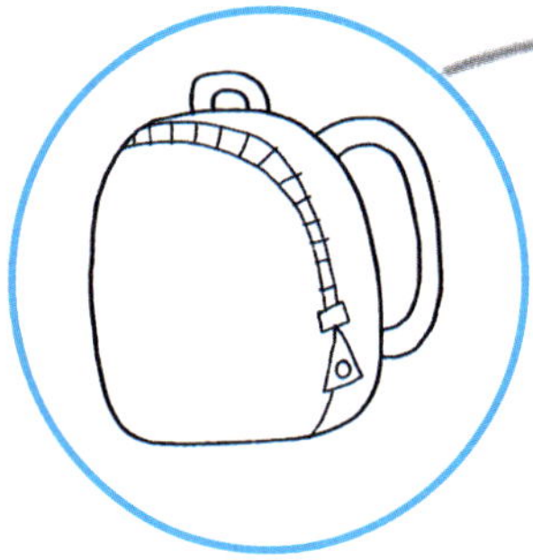

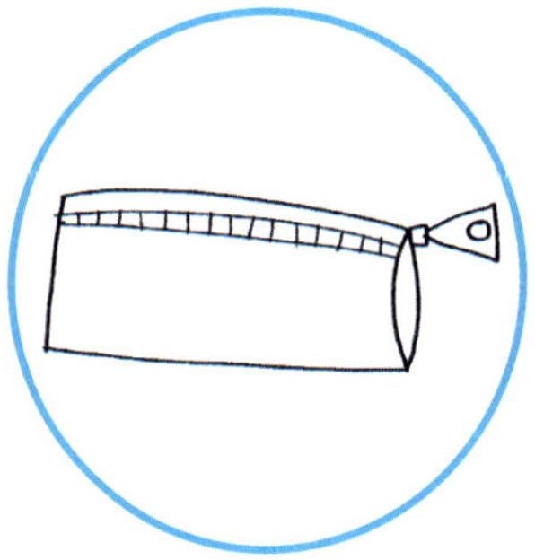

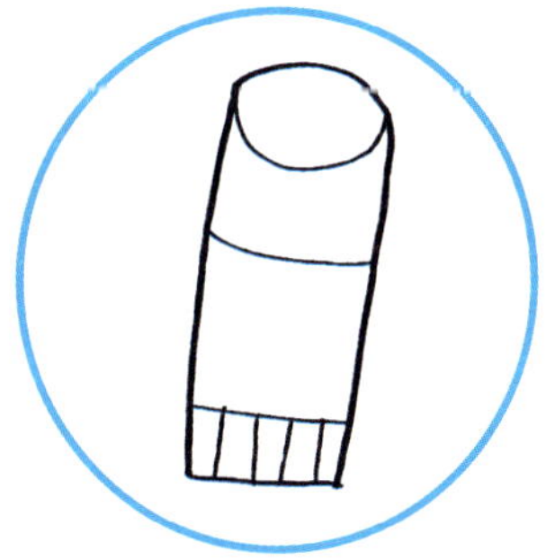

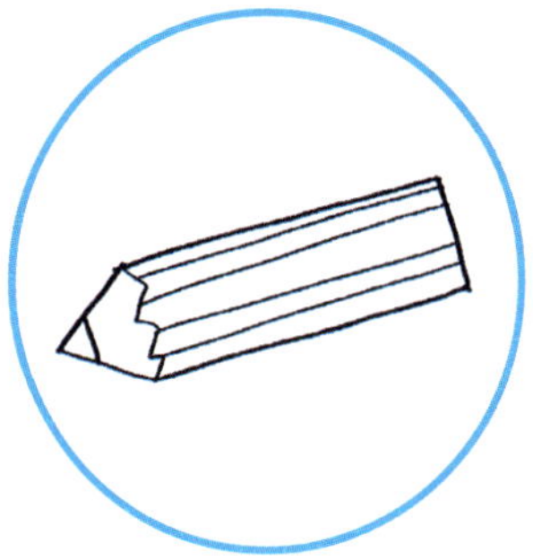

Look, find and match. Color the objects in your classroom. Point and say.
Language: backpack, crayons, glue, pencil, pencil case, scissors

Find and match the objects in the backpack. Color. Ask and say.

Language: backpack, crayons, glue, paints, paper, pencil, pencil case, scissors; Do you have your (backpack)? Yes, I do. / No, I don't.

1 2 3 4

Trace and say the numbers. Match to order the pictures. Circle your favorite picture.
Language: backpack, crayons, glue, paints, paper, pencil, pencil case, scissors; numbers 1–4

Color or paint Dylan and Mimi's pictures from the story. Ask and say.
Language: colors; Do you have (red) in your picture? Yes, I do. / No, I don't. I have (blue) in my picture.

Speaking

Life skills

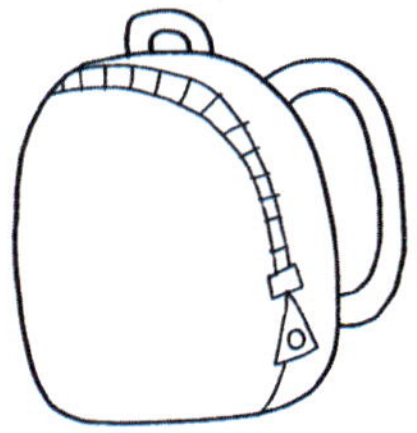

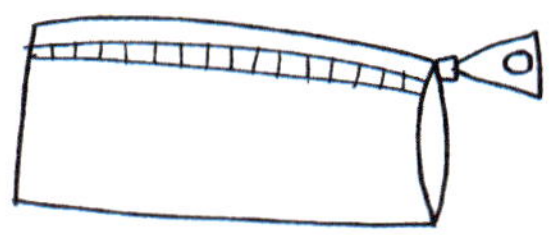

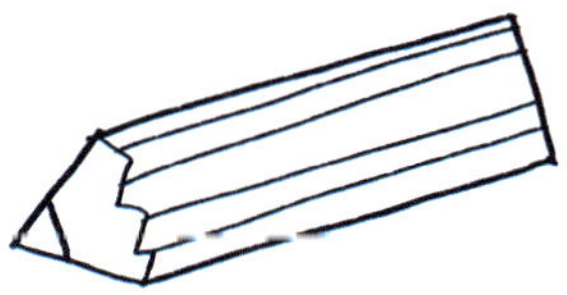

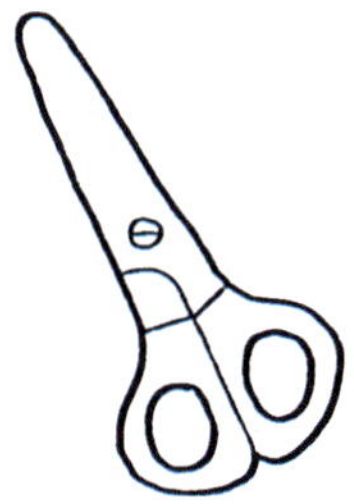

✔

✘

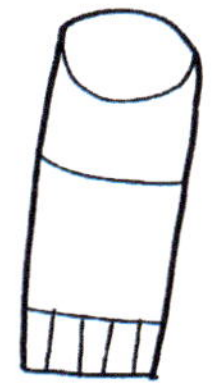

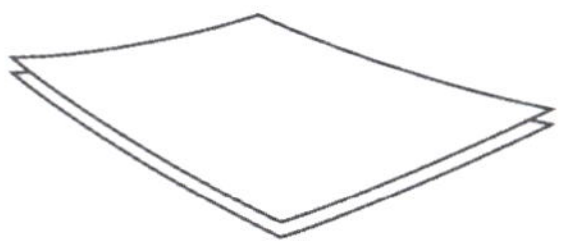

Draw and color the classroom objects you have (✔) and don't have (✘). Ask and say.

Language: backpack, crayons, glue, paints, paper, pencil, pencil case, scissors; Do you have (a backpack)? Yes, I do / No, I don't. I have (a pencil). I don't have (glue).

Values Good behavior

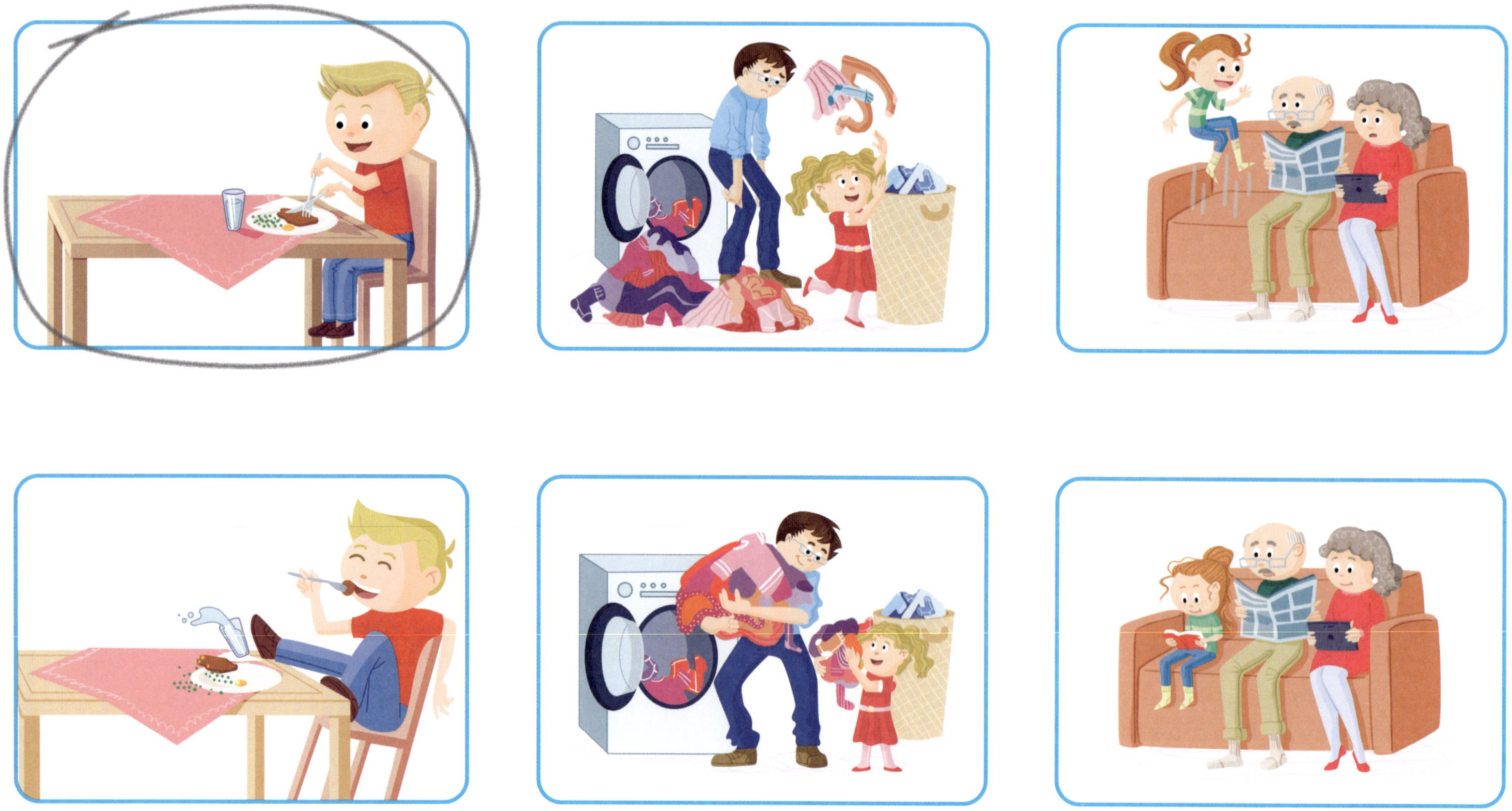

Circle the pictures of good behavior. Talk about you.
Language: daddy, grandma, grandpa; home, school; I'm good (at home/with my daddy).

Match the children to the places at school. Draw and color a picture of you in your favorite place in school. Say.
Language: cafeteria, classroom, library, playground; I'm in the (cafeteria).

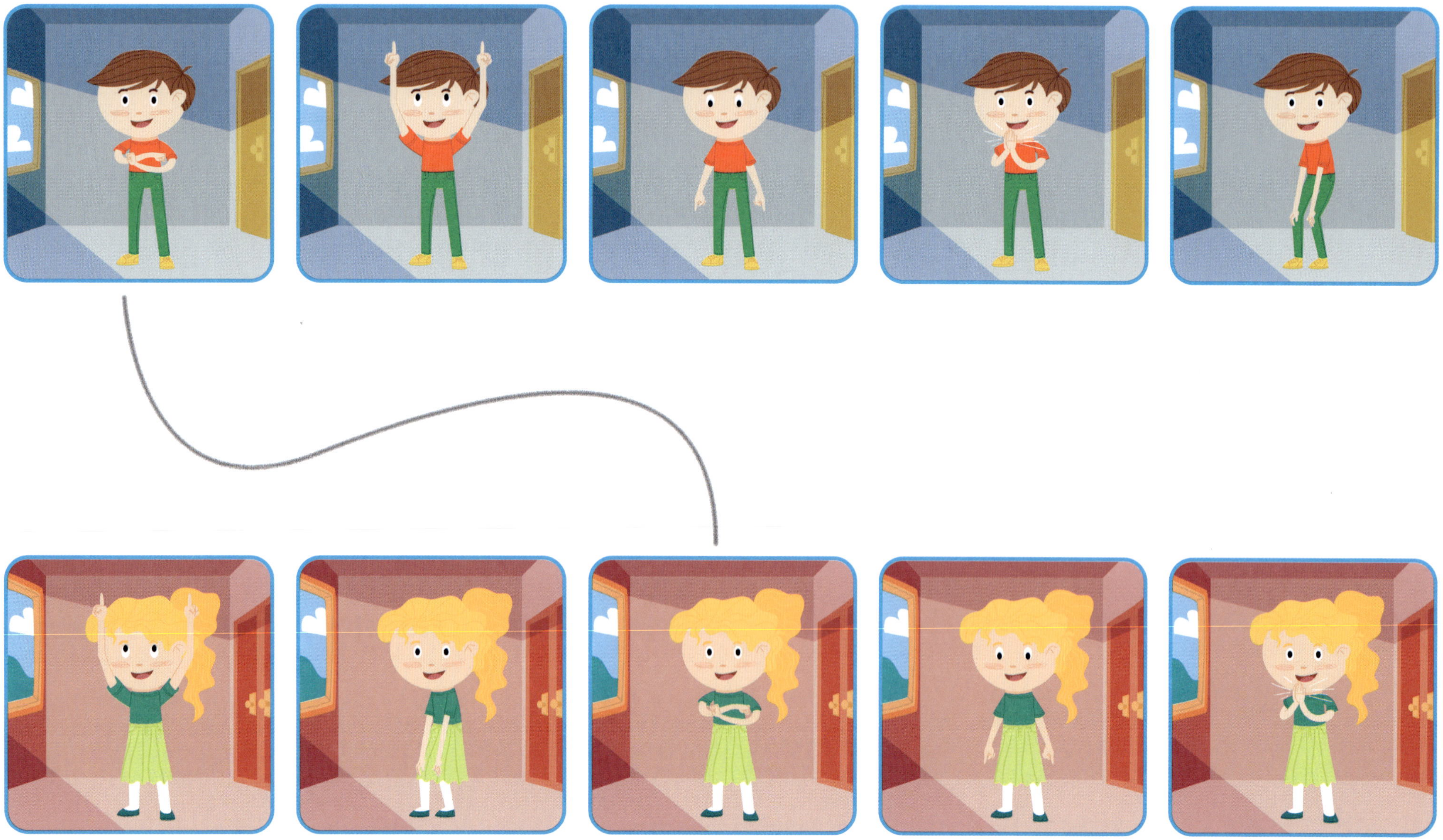

Match the children doing the actions for *Wind the bobbin up*. Point and say.

Language: ceiling, clap, floor, hands, knee; Point to the (ceiling). Clap your hands. Put your hands on your knee.

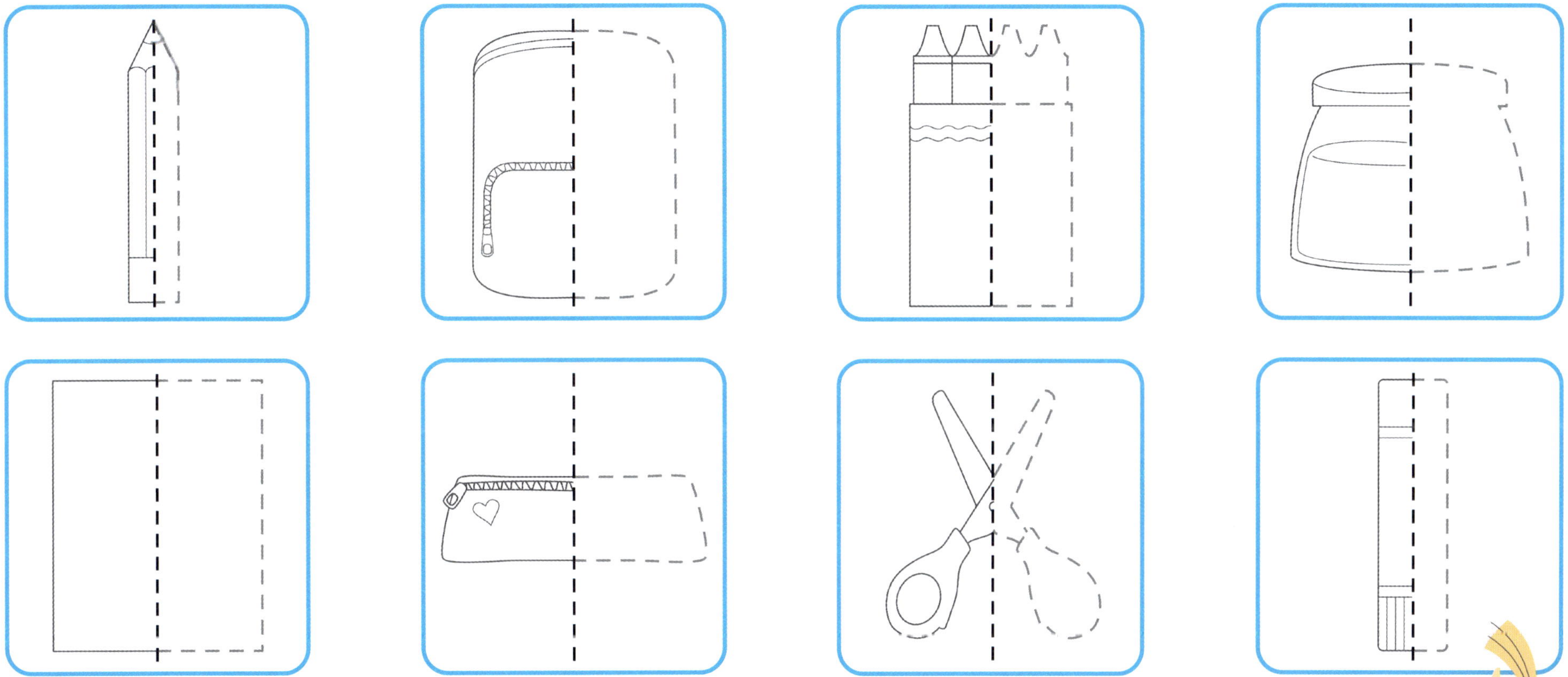

Trace and draw to complete the pictures. Choose and color two objects you have. Ask and say. Think and circle the number to show your progress. Language: backpack, crayons, glue, paints, paper, pencil, pencil case, scissors; Do you have (a pencil)? Yes, I do. / No, I don't. I have (crayons). I don't have (scissors).

Project

Use finger paints to paint the classroom objects. Point and say the colors. Talk about the classroom objects you have and don't have. **Language:** backpack, crayons, glue, paints, paper, pencil, pencil case, scissors; colors; The (pencil case) is (red). Do you have (a backpack)? Yes, I do. / No, I don't. I have (crayons). I don't have (scissors).

My body

I can dance!

Trace Mimi. Point and say. Color Mimi.
Language: arms, feet, hands, head, legs, tummy

Circle what you can do. Point and say.

Language: arms, feet, fingers, hands, head, legs, toes, tummy; I can/can't move my (head). Can you?

Trace and color Mimi. Point and say. Trace the ✔ or ✘ to show if Mimi can or can't dance.
Language: arms, feet, head, legs; I can move my (head). I can (dance).

Draw and color a picture of you dancing. Point and say.

Language: arms, feet, head, legs; Move your (head). I can move my (legs). I can (dance).

Match to show what you can (✓) and can't (✗) do. Ask and say.
Language: arms, feet, hands, head, legs, tummy; Can you move your (head)? Yes, I can. / No, I can't. What can you do? I can move my (feet).

Lesson 6 Values Making an effort

Match the missing objects to the children. Color to show what you can do if you try. Point and say.
Language: coat, scissors, shoes; I can/can't put on my (shoes). I can/can't cut with scissors.

Match the children doing the same actions. Color the circles green to show what you can do and red to show what you can't do. Ask and say.

Language: climb, hop, jump, run; What can you do? Can you (run)? Yes, I can. / No, I can't. I can/can't (climb).

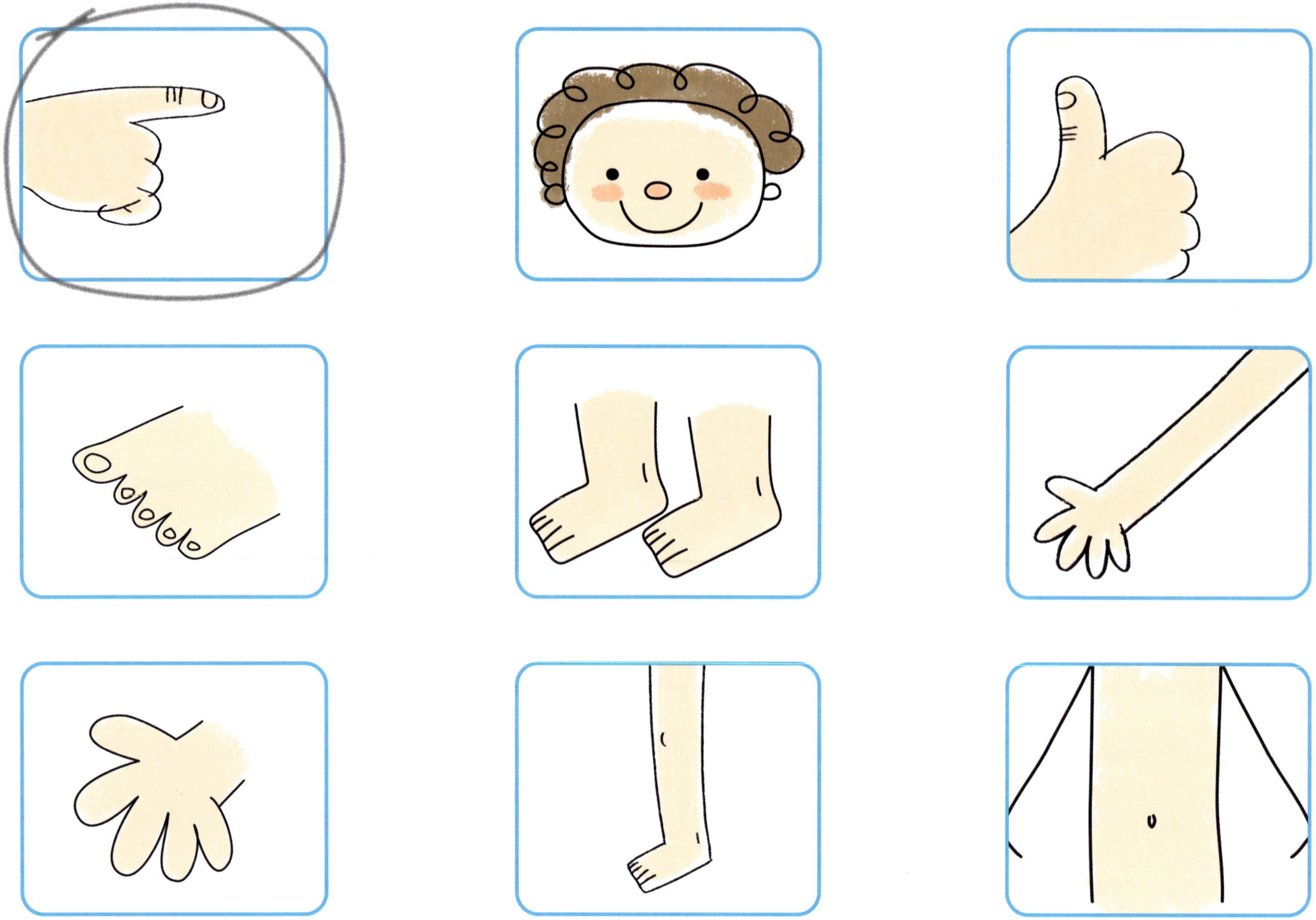

Circle the parts of the body in *One finger, one thumb, keep moving*. Point and say.
Language: arm, feet, finger, hand, head, leg, thumb, toes, tummy

hello

Choose and draw your face on four of the bodies to show what you can do. Ask and say. Think and circle the number to show your progress. Language: arms, feet, fingers, hands, head, legs, toes, tummy; Can you move your (head)? Yes, I can. / No, I can't. What can you do? I can/can't move my (legs).

6 8 10

Trace and paint the hands. Count your fingers and circle the correct number. Say.
Language: fingers, hands; colors; numbers 1–10; I have (ten) (fingers). The hands are (blue).

Clothes

Let's dress up!

Color the clothes following the key. Point and say.
Language: coat, dress, pants, shirt, skirt, sweater; colors; numbers 1-6

Follow and draw the paths from the children to the clothes. Color the clothes. Point and say.
Language: dress, pants, shirt, shoes, socks, sweater; colors; This is my (dress). These are my (pants). I'm wearing my (shoes).

1 2 3 4

Trace and say the numbers. Match to order the pictures. Circle your favorite picture.
Language: hat, pants, shirt, shoes, shorts; numbers 1–4; colors

Trace and color the clothes Mimi and Dylan wear to the party. Say.
Language: hat, pants, shirt, shoes, shorts; colors; I'm wearing (a green) (hat).

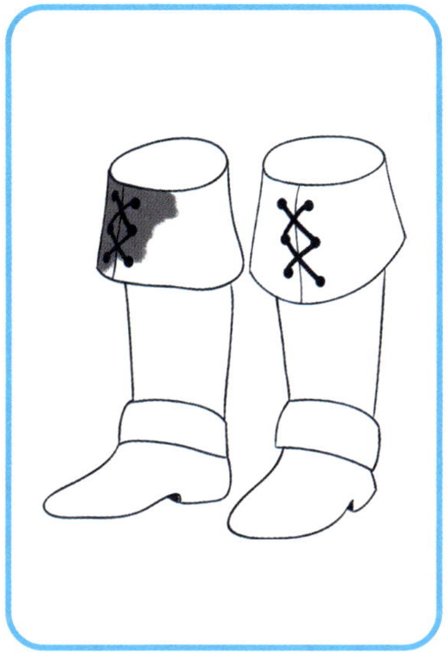

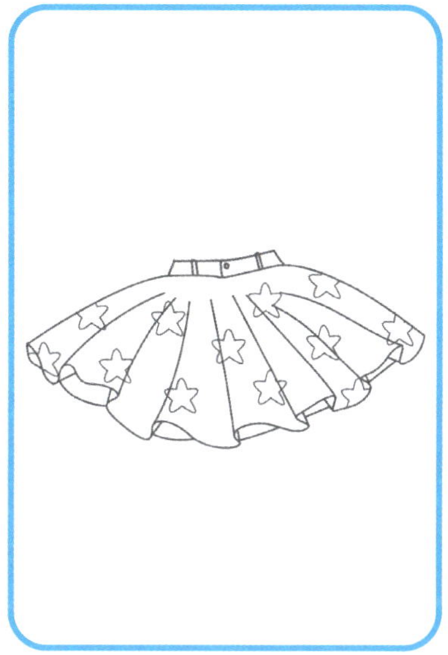

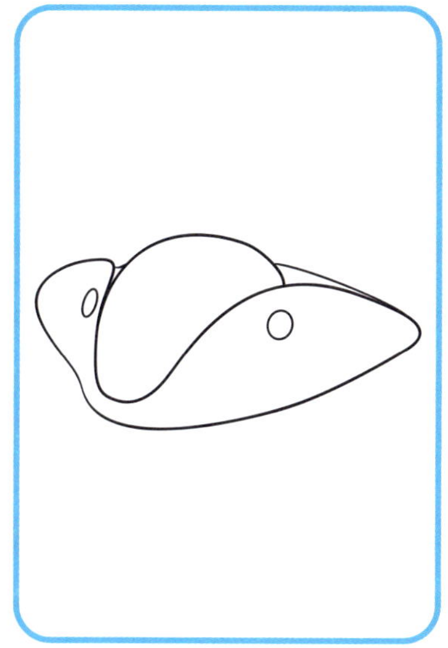

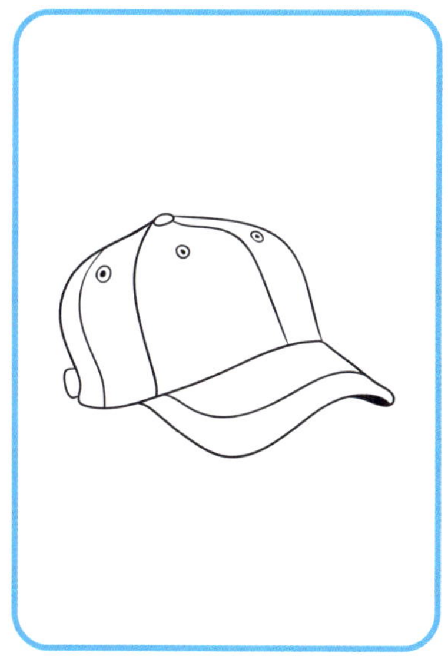

Find and color Uncle Dan's pirate clothes. Choose and circle clothes for you. Ask and say.
Language: boots, coat, dress, hat, pants, skirt; colors; What are you wearing? I'm wearing (green) (pants).

Values Cooperating

Circle the pictures of children cooperating. Talk about you.
Language: learn, play, share; family, friends; I (learn) with my (friends).

SOCIAL AND EMOTIONAL LEARNING

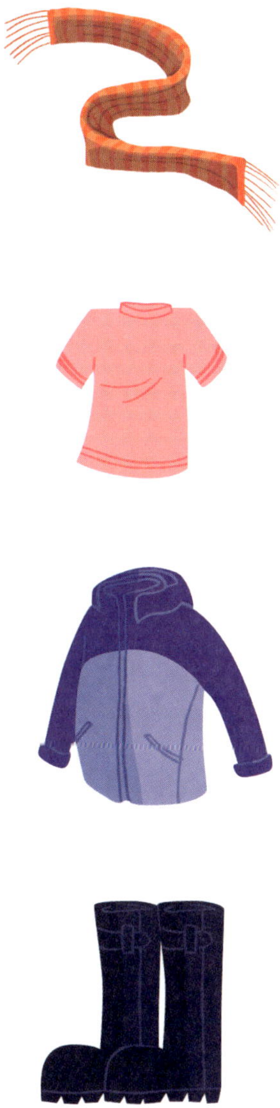

Draw clothes for hot and cold weather. Choose, ask and say.

Language: boots, coat, gloves, hat, sandals, scarf, shorts, T-shirt; cold, hot; It's (cold). What are you wearing? I'm wearing (a scarf).

Choose, draw and color your clothes. Mime and say.
Language: pants, shirt, shoes, skirt, socks, sweater; colors; This is the way I put on my (shirt).
What are you wearing? I'm wearing (a blue) (sweater).

Review

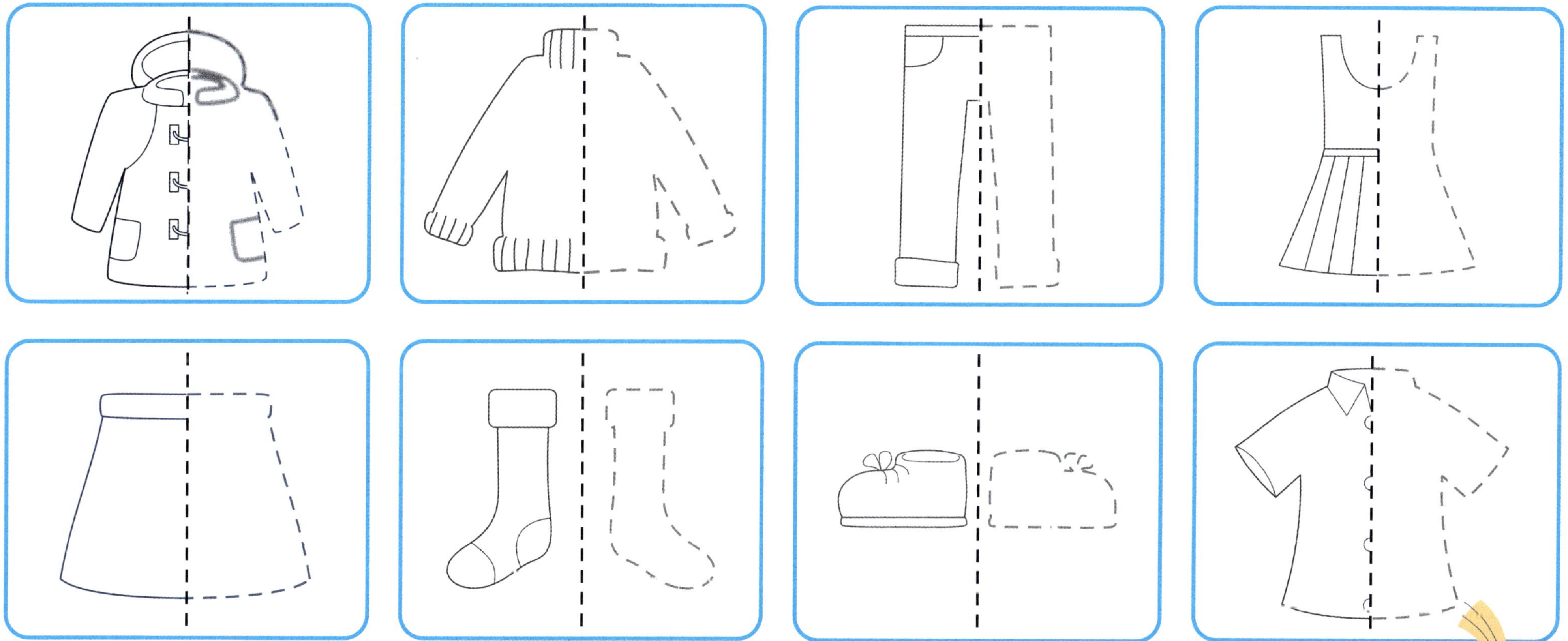

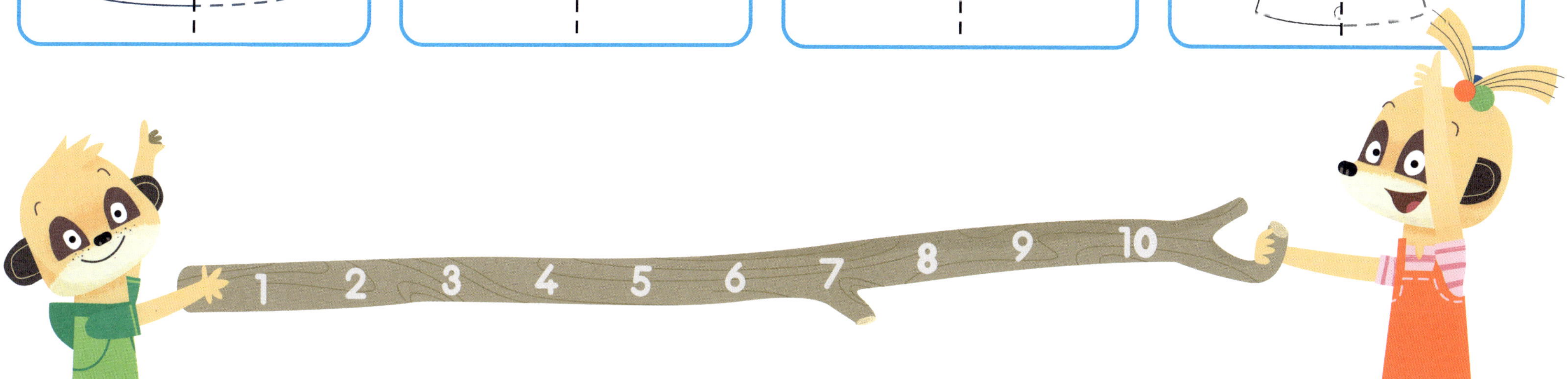

Trace and draw to complete the pictures. Choose and color four clothes for you. Ask and say. Think and circle the number to show your progress. Language: coat, dress, pants, shirt, shoes, skirt, socks, sweater; colors; This is my (skirt). These are my (shoes). What are you wearing? I'm wearing (a blue) (skirt).

Find and glue photos of you wearing clothes for hot weather and clothes for cold weather. Ask and say.
Language: boots, coat, dress, gloves, hat, pants, sandals, scarf, shirt, shoes, shorts, skirt, socks, sweater, T-shirt; cold, hot; colors; It's (cold). What are you wearing? I'm wearing (green) (gloves).

Match the meerkats to the places. Color the pictures that show what you do at home. Point and say.
Language: bathroom, bedroom, dining room, house, kitchen, living room

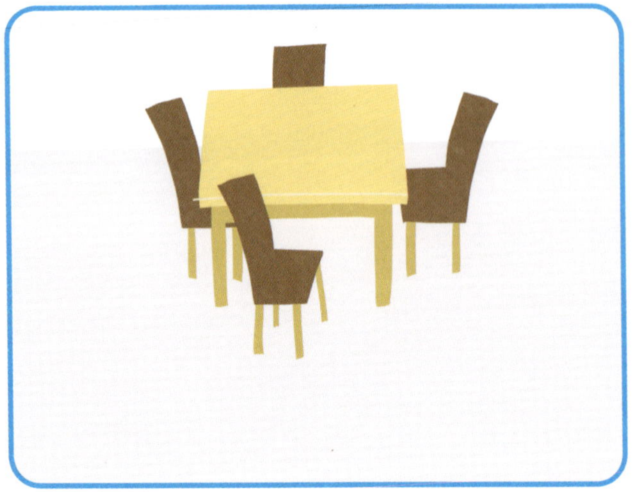

hello

Draw the boy and girl in different places. Ask and say.
Language: bedroom, dining room, garage, kitchen, living room, yard; Is he/she in the (yard)? Yes. / No.

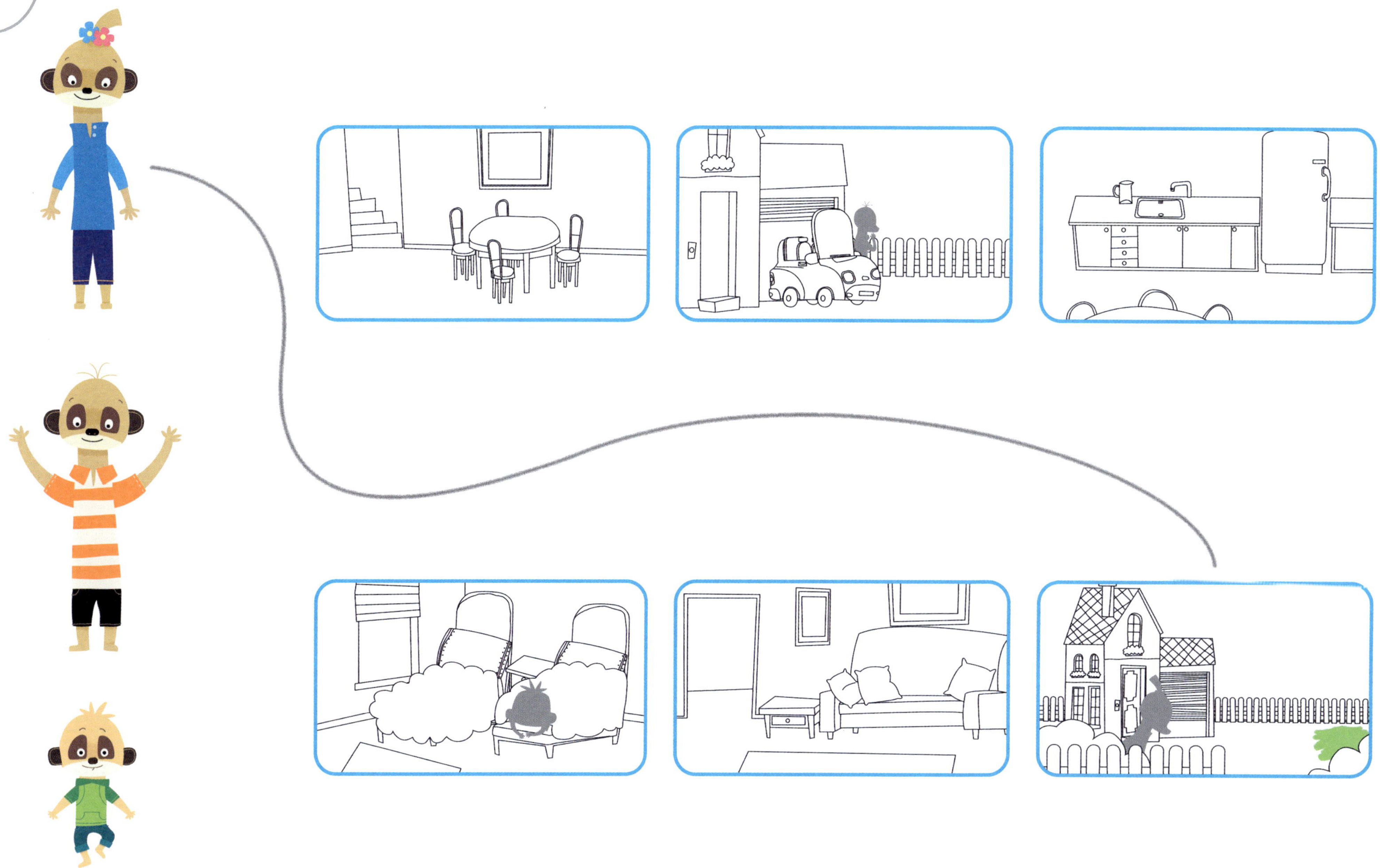

Match Mommy, Daddy and Dylan to their hiding places. Color the hiding places. Ask and say.

Language: bedroom, dining room, garage, kitchen, living room, yard; Is (Mommy) in the (garage)? Yes, he/she is. / No, he/she isn't.

Follow and draw the path from Mommy, Daddy and Mimi to Dylan. Ask and say.

Language: bedroom, dining room, kitchen, living room; Is Dylan in the (kitchen)? Yes, he is. / No, he isn't. Where's Dylan? In the (bedroom).

hello

Find and circle Bruno the dog and Kitty the cat. Say.
Language: bedroom, bathroom, dining room, garage, house, kitchen, living room, yard; cat, dog; He's/She's in the (garage). He/She isn't in the (yard).

Values Families are different

Match the pictures with the same family members. Name the family members. Point and say.
Language: family, mommy, daddy, brother, sister, grandma, grandpa; big, small; This family is (big).

SOCIAL AND EMOTIONAL LEARNING

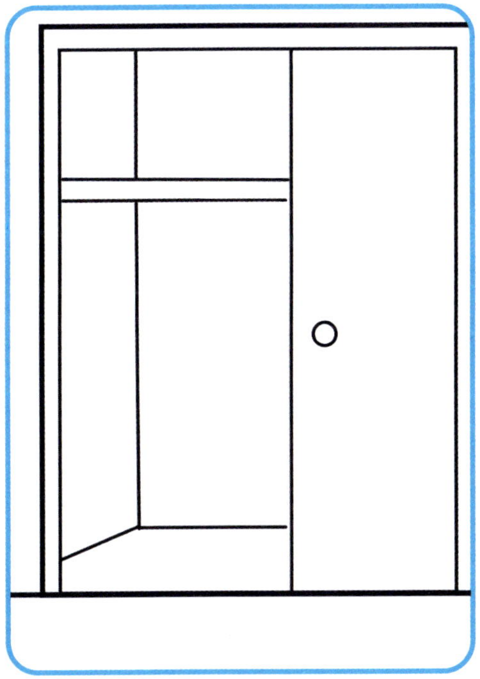

Draw and color the things in the correct places. Say.

Language: box, closet, recycling bin, shelf; books, clothes, paper, toys; I put (paper) (in) the (recycling bin).

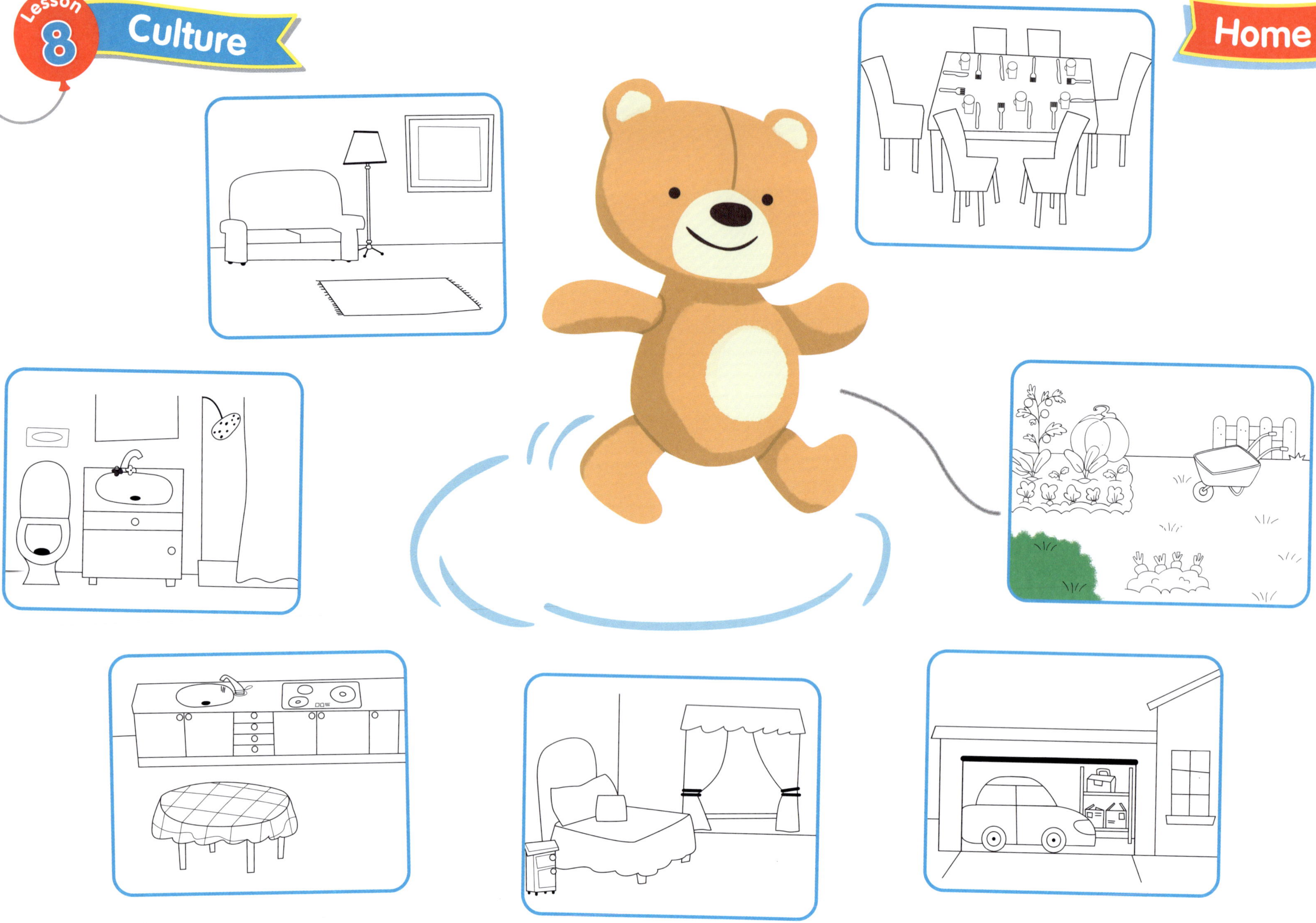

Match the teddy bear to the places in the song. Color the places in the song. Point and say.

Language: teddy bear; bathroom, bedroom, dining room, garage, garden, kitchen, living room; Round and round the (garden).

Draw Mimi, Dylan, Mommy and Daddy in four different places. Ask and say. Think and circle the number to show your progress.
Language: bathroom, bedroom, dining room, garage, house, kitchen, living room, yard; Where's (Mimi)? He's/She's in the (garage). He/She isn't in the (yard). Is (Daddy) in the (bathroom)? Yes, he/she is. / No, he/she isn't.

Trace the rectangles. Decorate and paint your ideal bedroom. Say.
Language: bedroom; big, small; colors; This is my (bedroom). It's (big/blue).

Food

I like ice cream!

Vocabulary

Lesson 1

Look, find and match. Trace and color. Point and say.

Language: apples, bread, cereal, eggs, ice cream, milk

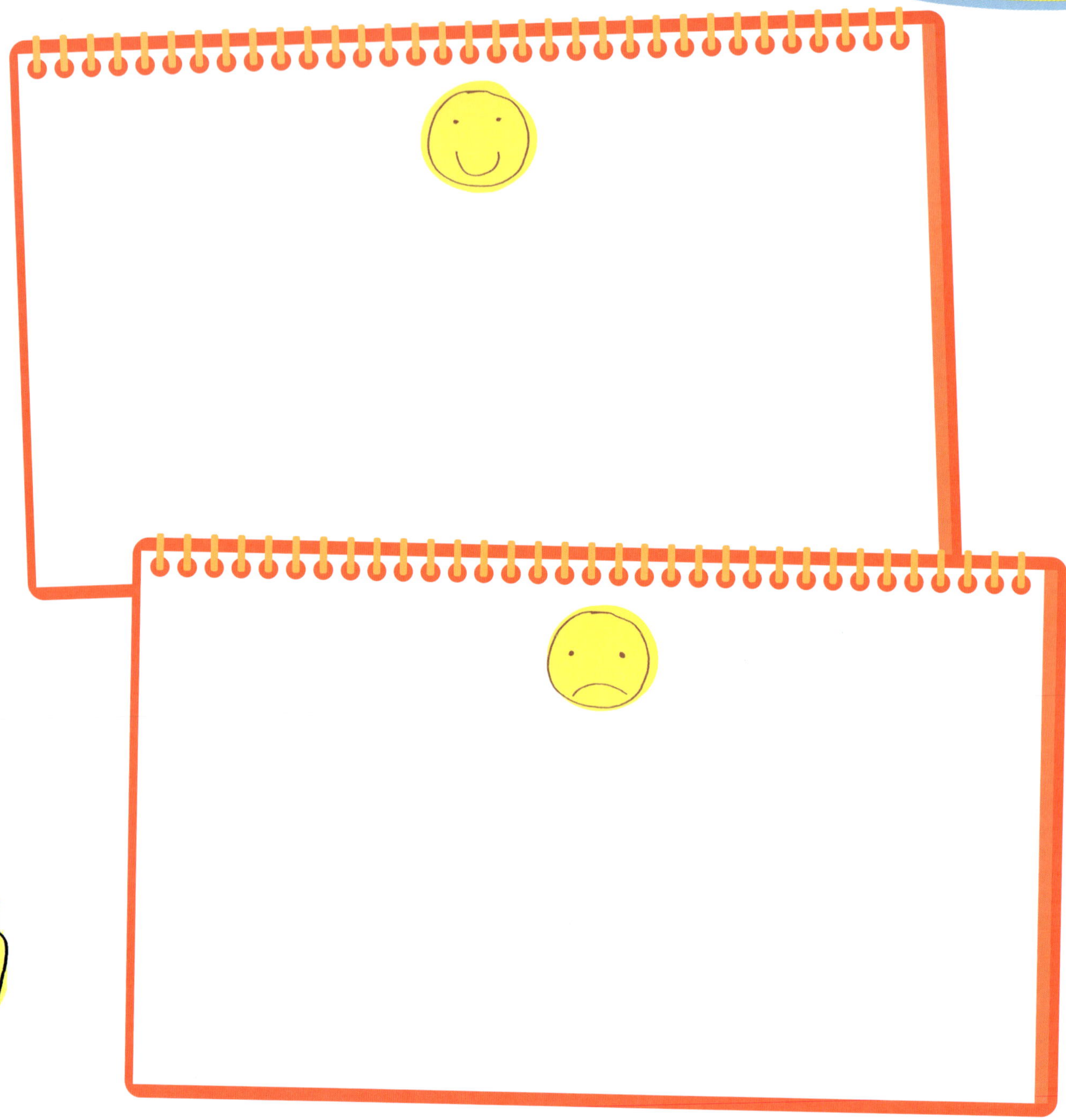

Draw and color two foods you like and two foods you don't like. Say.

Language: apples, bananas, bread, carrots, cereal, eggs, ice cream, milk; I like (eggs). I don't like (bananas). How about you?

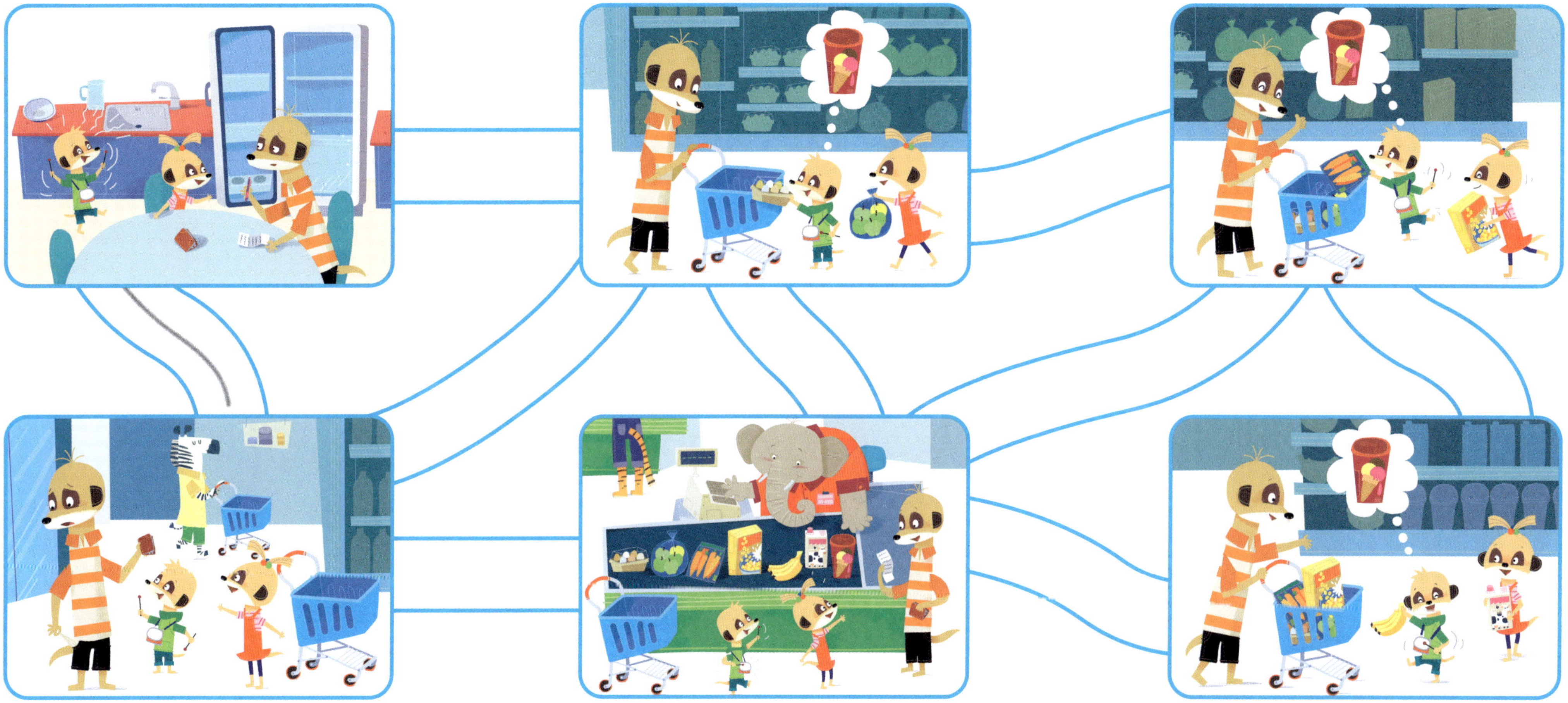

Draw lines to show the story sequence. Color the food Mimi, Dylan and Daddy buy.
Language: apples, bananas, bread, carrots, cereal, eggs, ice cream, milk

Story Song

Draw and color the next food in the sequence. Trace and color the ice cream. Point and say.
Language: apples, bananas, carrots, cereal, eggs, ice cream, milk

Trace and draw two pictures of you. Circle the food you like blue and color. Circle the food you don't like red. Match the food to the correct faces. Ask and say.

Language: apples, bananas, bread, carrots, cereal, eggs, ice cream, milk; Do you like (milk)? Yes, I do. / No I don't.

Circle the pictures of children helping. Talk about the people you help.
Language: mommy, daddy, brother, sister, friend, teacher; I help my (mommy).

SOCIAL AND EMOTIONAL LEARNING

Check (✓) and color the food that grows in the garden. Point and say.

Language: apples, bananas, bread, carrots, cereal, eggs, ice cream, milk, pears, peas, potatoes, tomatoes

15

20

Color and count the peas. Trace the numbers. Match the pictures to the numbers. Circle the hot peas pudding.
Language: peas, plate, pudding; hot, cold; numbers 1-20

Complete the faces to show food you like and food you don't like. Ask and say. Think and circle the number to show your progress.
Language: apples, bananas, bread, carrots, cereal, eggs, ice cream, milk; Do you like (eggs)? Yes, I do. / No, I don't. I like (carrots). I don't like (milk). How about you?

Use finger paints to paint the food. Point and say the colors. Talk about the food you like and don't like.
Language: apples, bananas, bread, carrots, cereal, eggs, ice cream, milk, pears, peas, potatoes, tomatoes; colors; I like (eggs). I don't like (apples). Do you like (carrots)? Yes, I do. / No, I don't.

Farm animals

Aunt Emma's farm

Draw and color the next animal in the sequence. Point and say.
Language: cow, dog, duck, goat, hen, sheep

Farm animals

Find and count the animals in the picture. Trace and circle the correct number for each animal. Ask and say.
Language: cow, duck, hen, horse, rooster, sheep; numbers 1-6; What animals are on the farm? There's a (rooster). How many (hens)? (Four).

Trace the ✓ and ✗ to show which animals are and aren't in the story. Color the animals in the story. Say.

Language: cow, dog, duck, goat, hen, horse, rooster, sheep; There's a (sheep).

Match and color the animals. Point and say the animal noises.
Language: cow, duck, rooster, sheep; animal noises; The (cow) goes (moo).

Find and circle four differences. Color the frame of the picture which shows the farm from the video. Say.
Language: cow, dog, duck, goat, hen, horse, rooster, sheep; There's a (dog). There are (hens).

Values Being kind to animals

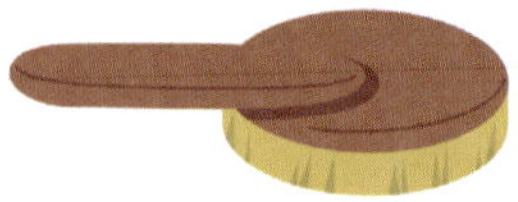

Match the objects to the pictures of a child being kind to animals. Point and say.
Language: cow, dog, hen, horse; clean, food, home, kind, water; I like (hens). I'm kind to animals.

SOCIAL AND EMOTIONAL LEARNING

Lesson 7

Content

Farm animals

Draw the babies next to the animals. Say.
Language: cow, calf, dog, puppy, horse, foal, sheep, lamb; This is a (cow). The baby is a (calf).

14 20 18

Color the little ducks yellow. Count the little ducks and trace the correct number. Say.

Language: duck; yellow; numbers 1-20; There are (twenty) little ducks.

Choose and color the farm animals you want to play with. Ask and say. Think and circle the number to show your progress.
Language: cow, dog, duck, goat, hen, horse, rooster, sheep; There's a (cow). There are (ducks). How many (hens)? (Three).

Project

Draw a picture of you. Choose and draw animals for your farm. Color or paint the farm. Say.
Language: cow, dog, duck, goat, hen, horse, rooster, sheep; colors; numbers; There's a (sheep). There are (six) (ducks). My (horse) is (black). How many (ducks)? (Four).

Transportation

Let's go by bike!

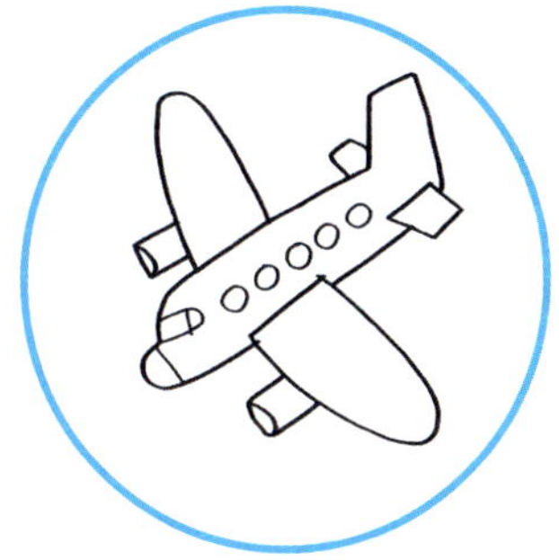

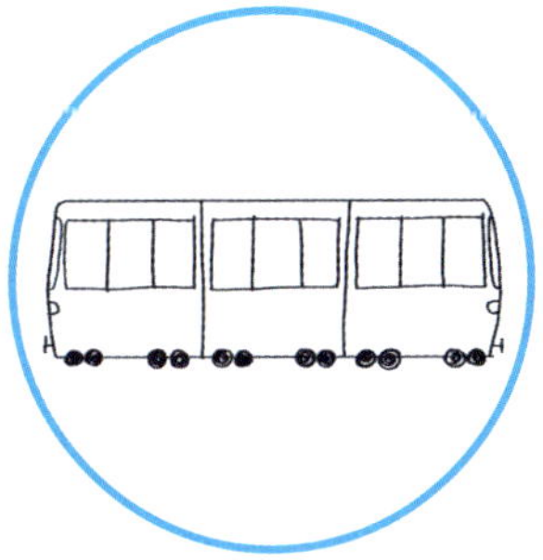

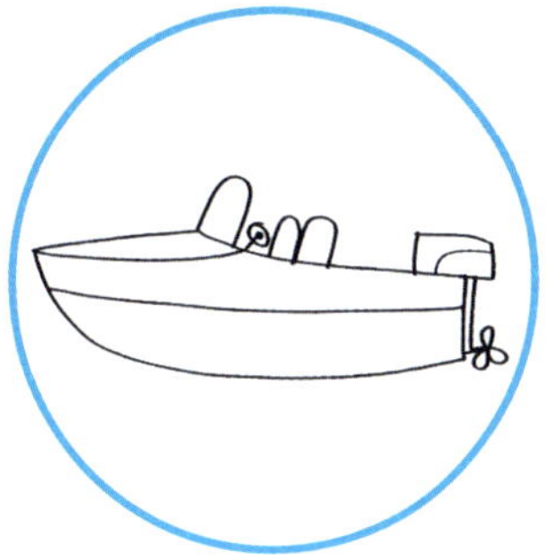

Look, find and match. Color. Point and say.

Language: bike, boat, bus, car, plane, train

Choose and color the transport you want to use. Point and say.

Language: bike, boat, bus, car, motorcycle, plane, train, truck; Let's go by (bus)! Yes. / No.

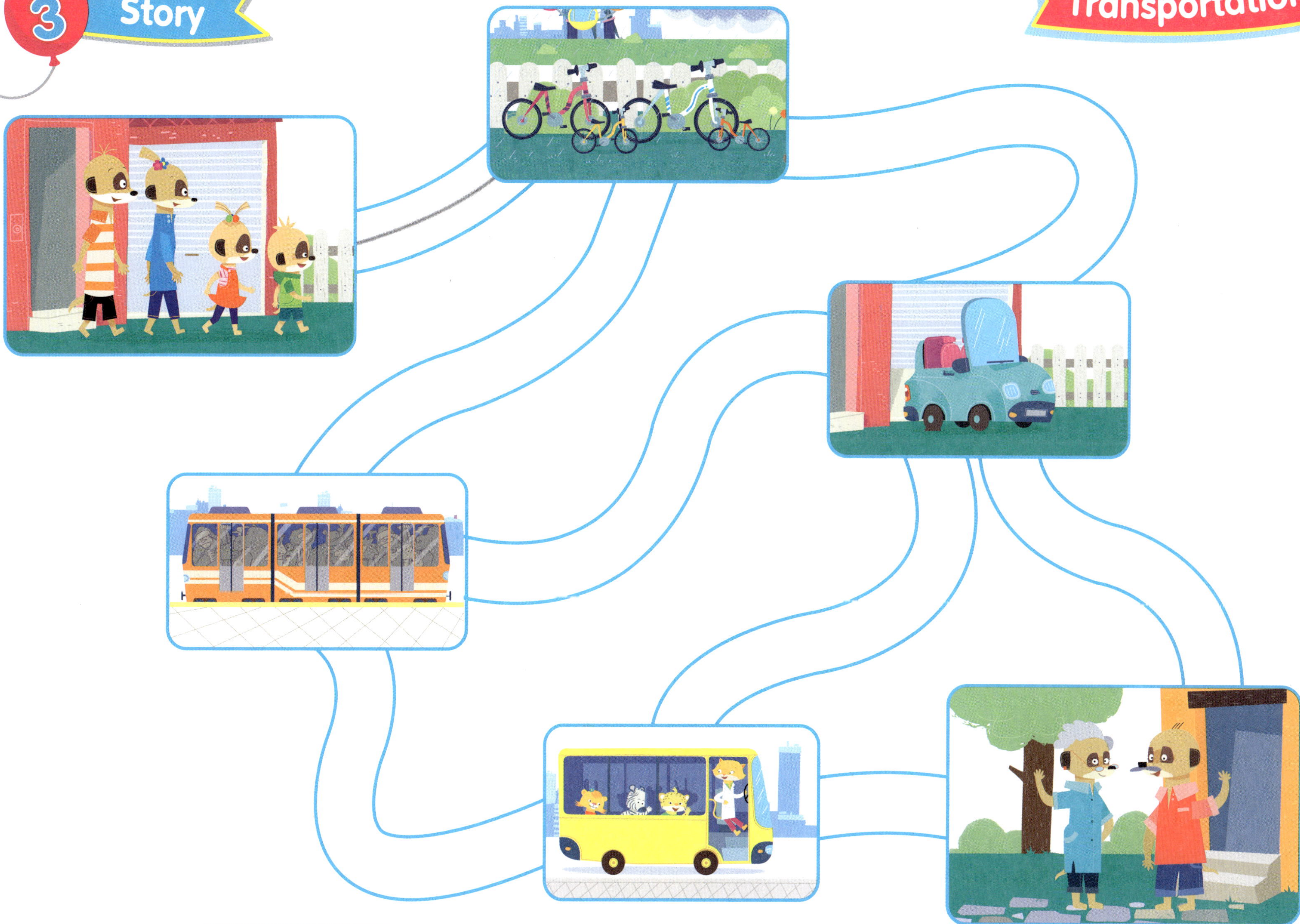

Draw lines to show the order of the transportation in the story. Point and say.
Language: bike, bus, car, train; Let's go by (bike). I want to go by (car).

Match the puzzle pieces. Circle the two puzzle pieces with the transportation the meerkats use in the story. Point and say.

Language: bike, bus, car, train; Let's go by (bike). I want to go by (car).

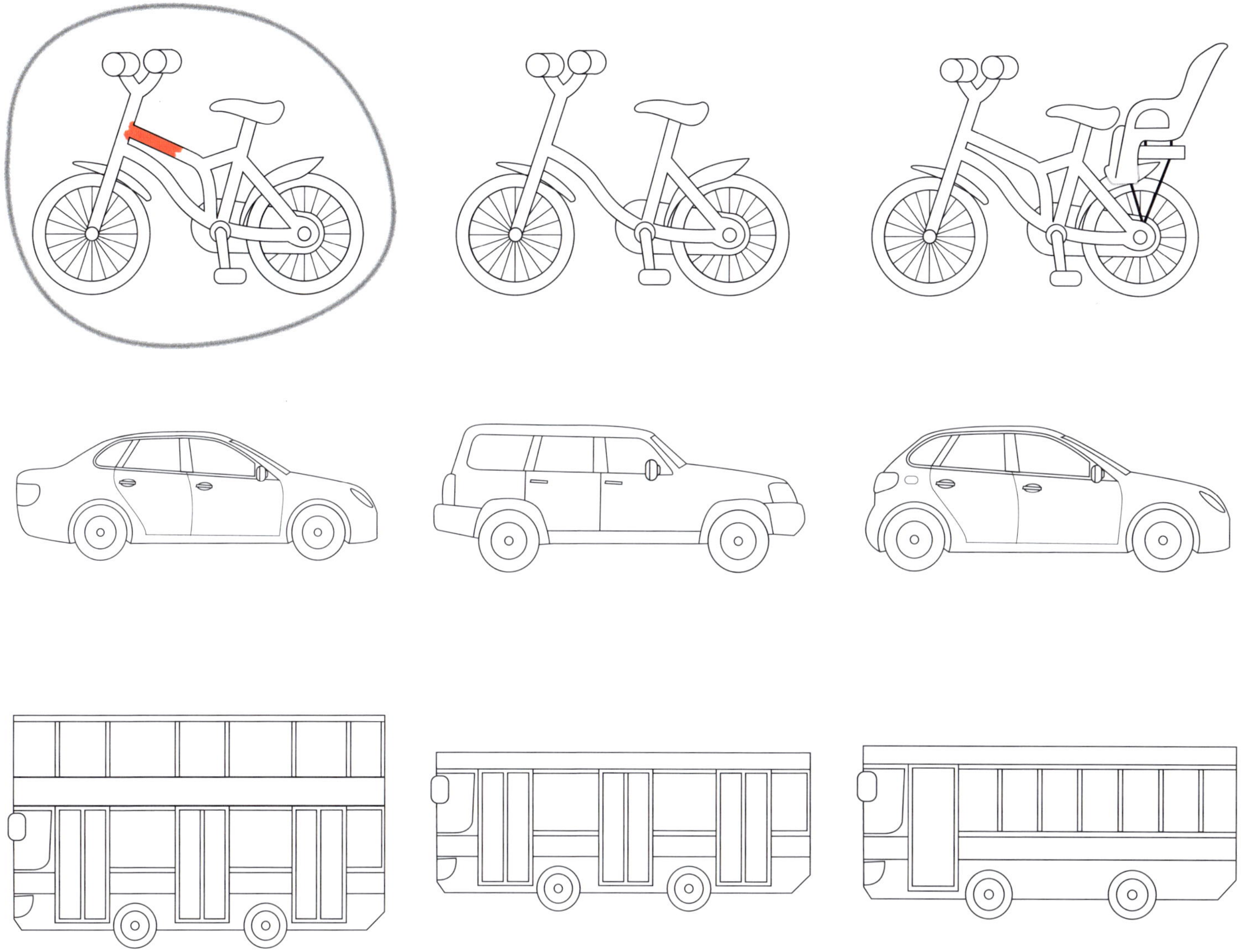

Find and circle the pictures which are the same. Color. Ask and say.
Language: bike, bus, car; Do you want to go by (bus)? Yes, I do. / No, I don't.

Values Thinking of others

Check (✓) the pictures which show children thinking of others. Choose and color one picture to show how you think of others. Say.

Language: mommy, daddy, brother, sister, friend; I think of my (daddy). I say please/sorry/thank you.

Draw the transportation in the correct places. Say.

Language: air, road, track, water; boat, bus, motorcycle, plane, train; A (bus) goes (on the road). A (plane) goes (in the air).

Trace the paths. Color your favorite rowing boat. Say.
Language: boat, dream, row, stream; Row, row, row your boat.

Transportation

Draw yourself on your favorite forms of transportation. Ask and say. Think and circle the number to show your progress. Language: bike, boat, bus, car, motorcycle, plane, train, truck; Let's go by (bus)! Yes. / No. I want to go by (bike). Do you want to go by (train)? Yes, I do. / No, I don't.

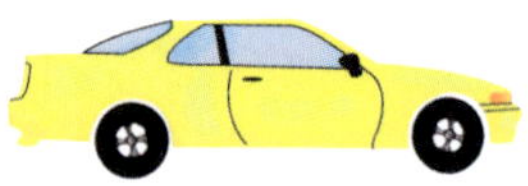

Find and glue pictures of transportation with wheels. Count and say.

Language: bike, bus, car, motorcycle, plane, scooter, train, truck; wheel; numbers; How many (wheels)? (Four.) This is a (truck). It has (ten) (wheels).

Follow and draw the path through the maze. Point and say.

Language: Earth, moon, planet, sky, star, sun

Match the pictures to the puzzle pieces. Color the pictures that are in the puzzle. Ask and say.
Language: astronaut, Earth, moon, planet, rocket, sky, star, sun; What's this? It's (a planet).

Find and circle four differences. Point and say. Color the spot under the picture from the story.
Language: astronaut, Earth, moon, planet, rocket, star; What's this? It's (a planet). Can you see (the moon)? Yes, I can. / No, I can't.

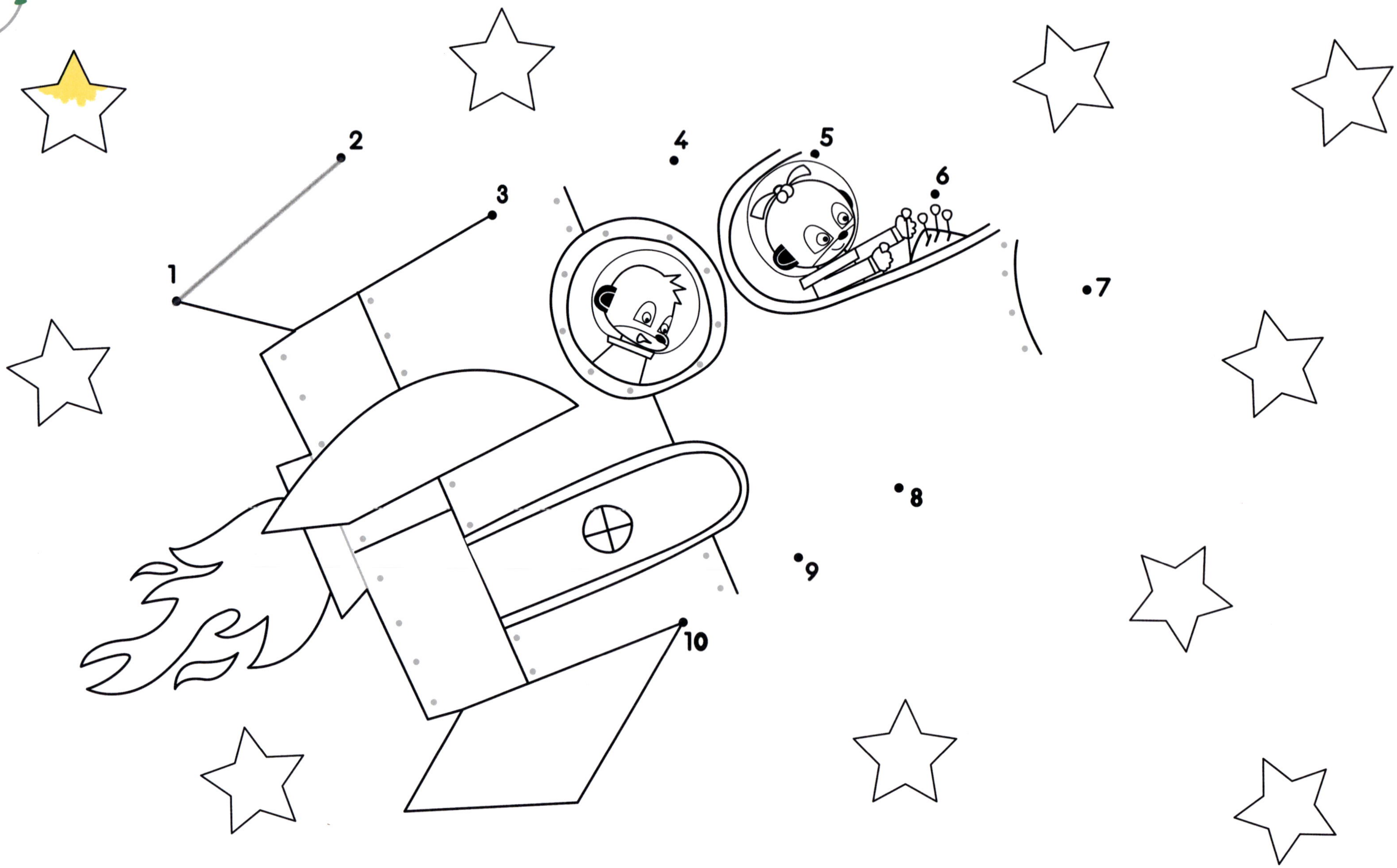

Count and connect the dots to complete the picture. Count and color the stars. Ask and say.
Language: moon, rocket, star; numbers 1–10; I can/can't see (the moon). Can you see (the rocket)? Yes, I can. / No, I can't. How many (stars)? (Ten).

Draw three more stars and one more planet. Color the picture. Count, ask and say.
Language: Earth, moon, planet, star, sun; numbers; What's this? It's (a planet). Can you see (the sun)? Yes, I can. / No, I can't. What can you see? I can see (three) (planets). How many (stars)? (Seven).

Lesson 6 Values Feelings

Match the feelings to the pictures. Say.
Language: angry, calm, happy, sad, scared, sleepy; Sometimes I'm (angry).

SOCIAL AND EMOTIONAL LEARNING

Draw the things you can see in the day and at night. Ask and say.

Language: day, night; clouds, moon, rainbow, sky, stars, sun; In the day, I can see (clouds). At night, I can see (the moon). Can you see (a rainbow) (at night)? Yes, I can. / No, I can't. What can you see (in the day)?

Match the pictures. Trace and color. Point, ask and say.
Language: cat, cow, dish, dog, moon, spoon; What's this? It's (a spoon).

Trace the paths. Color the pictures. Ask and say. Think and circle the number to show your progress.
Language: astronaut, Earth, moon, planet, rocket, sky, star, sun; What's this? It's (a star). What can you see?
I can see (an astronaut). Can you see (the moon)? Yes, I can. / No, I can't.

Draw a picture of you on the moon. Color the sun yellow, the Earth blue and the other planet red. Ask and say.
Language: astronaut, Earth, moon, planet, rocket, sky, star, sun; colors; What's this? It's (my rocket). It's (blue). What can you see? I can see (the Earth). Can you see (the sun)? Yes, I can. / No, I can't.

Colors

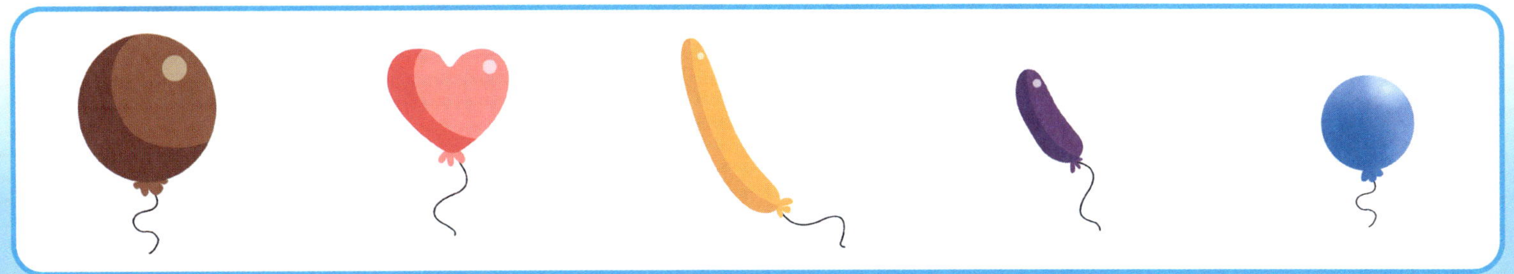

Color the balloons following the key. Point and say.
Language: blue, brown, orange, pink, purple

Colors

1
2
3
4
5

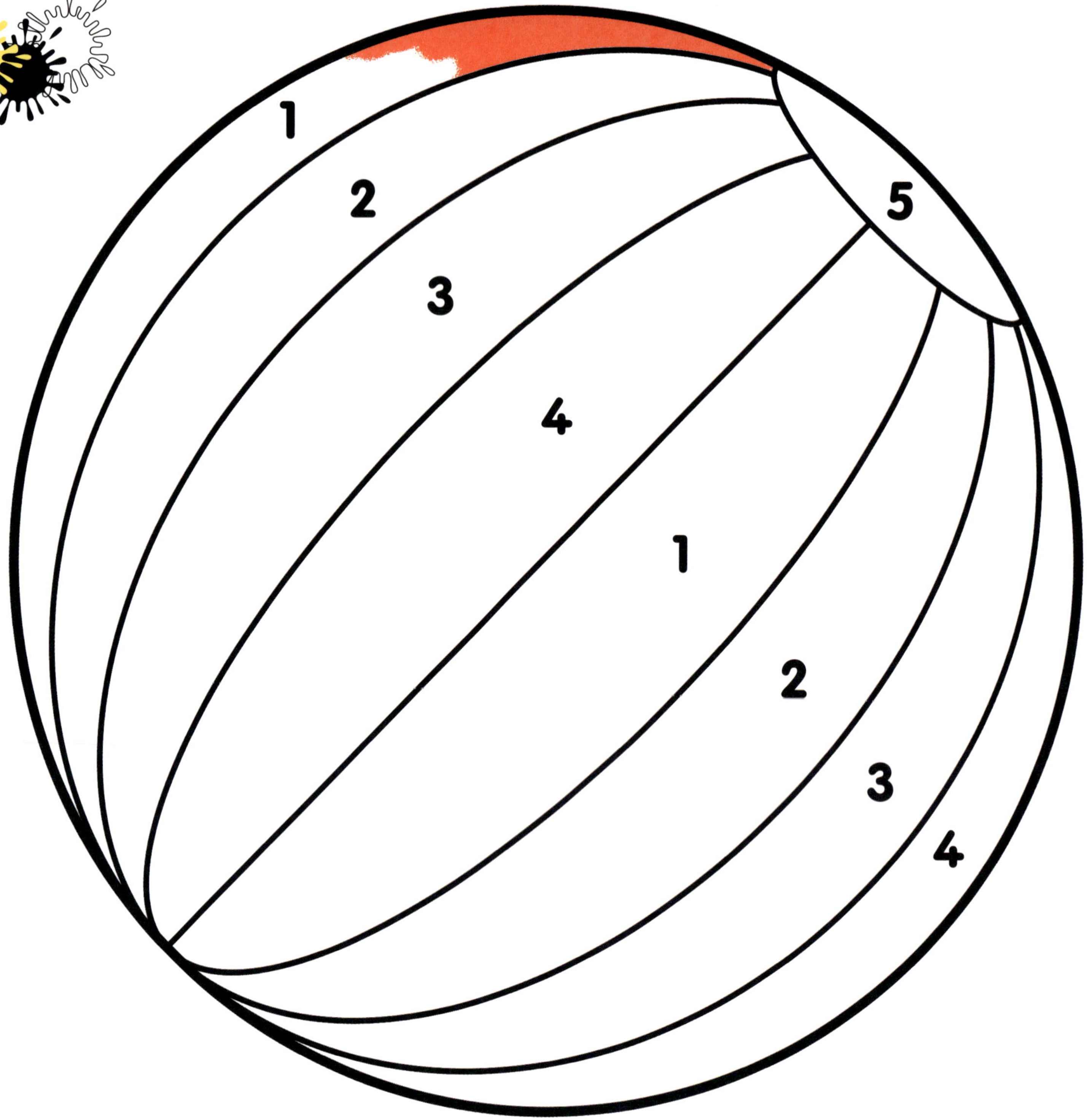

Color the ball following the key. Point and say.
Language: black, green, red, white, yellow; numbers 1–5

Numbers 123

1 2 3 4 5 6 7 8 9 10

11 12 13 14 15 16 17 18 19 20

Count and match each picture to the correct number. Point and say.
Language: numbers 1–20

Count and connect the dots to complete the picture. Color the picture. Point and say.
Language: numbers 1–20

Shapes

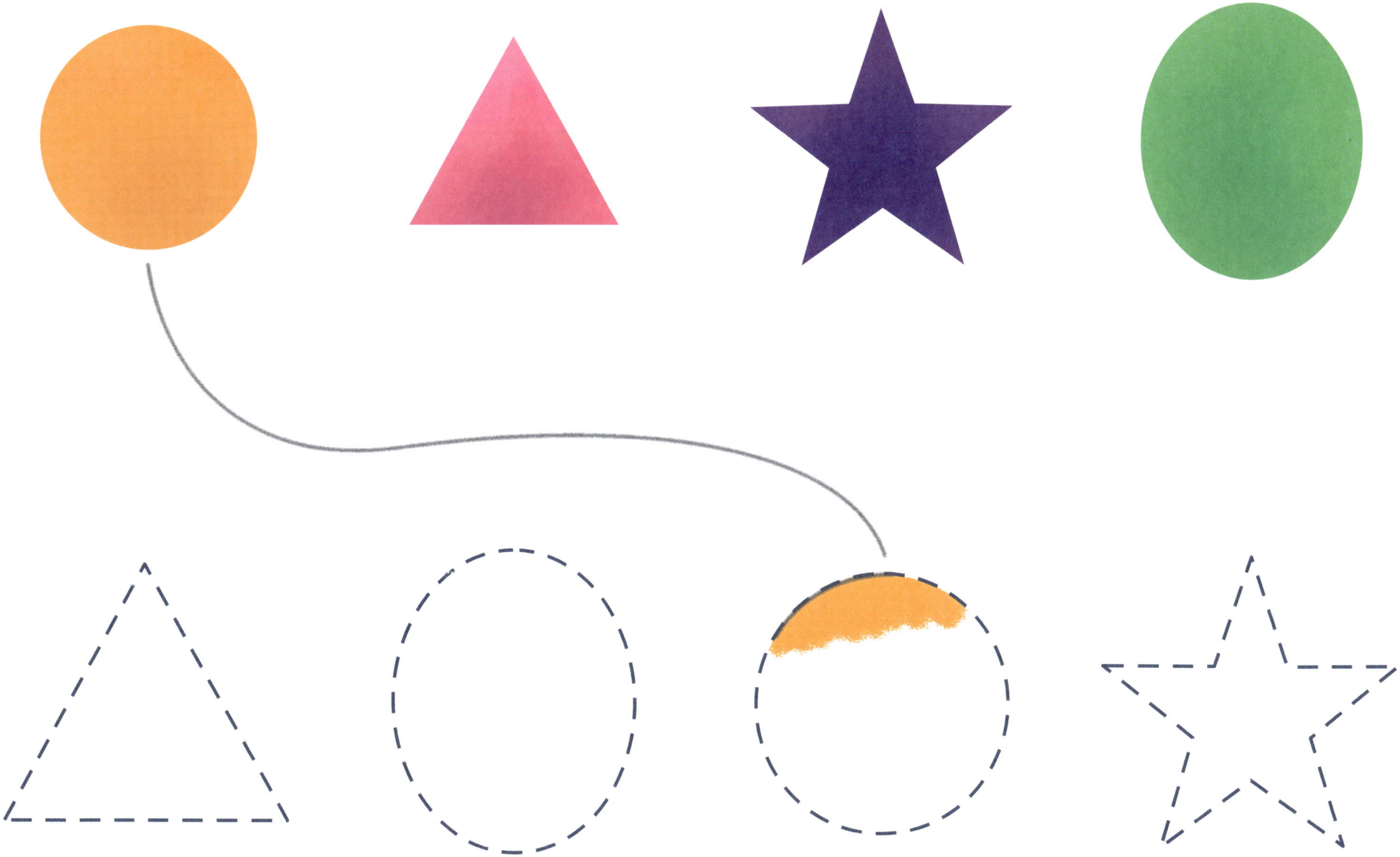

Match and trace the shapes. Color the shapes so they are the same. Point and say.
Language: circle, oval, star, triangle; colors

Shapes

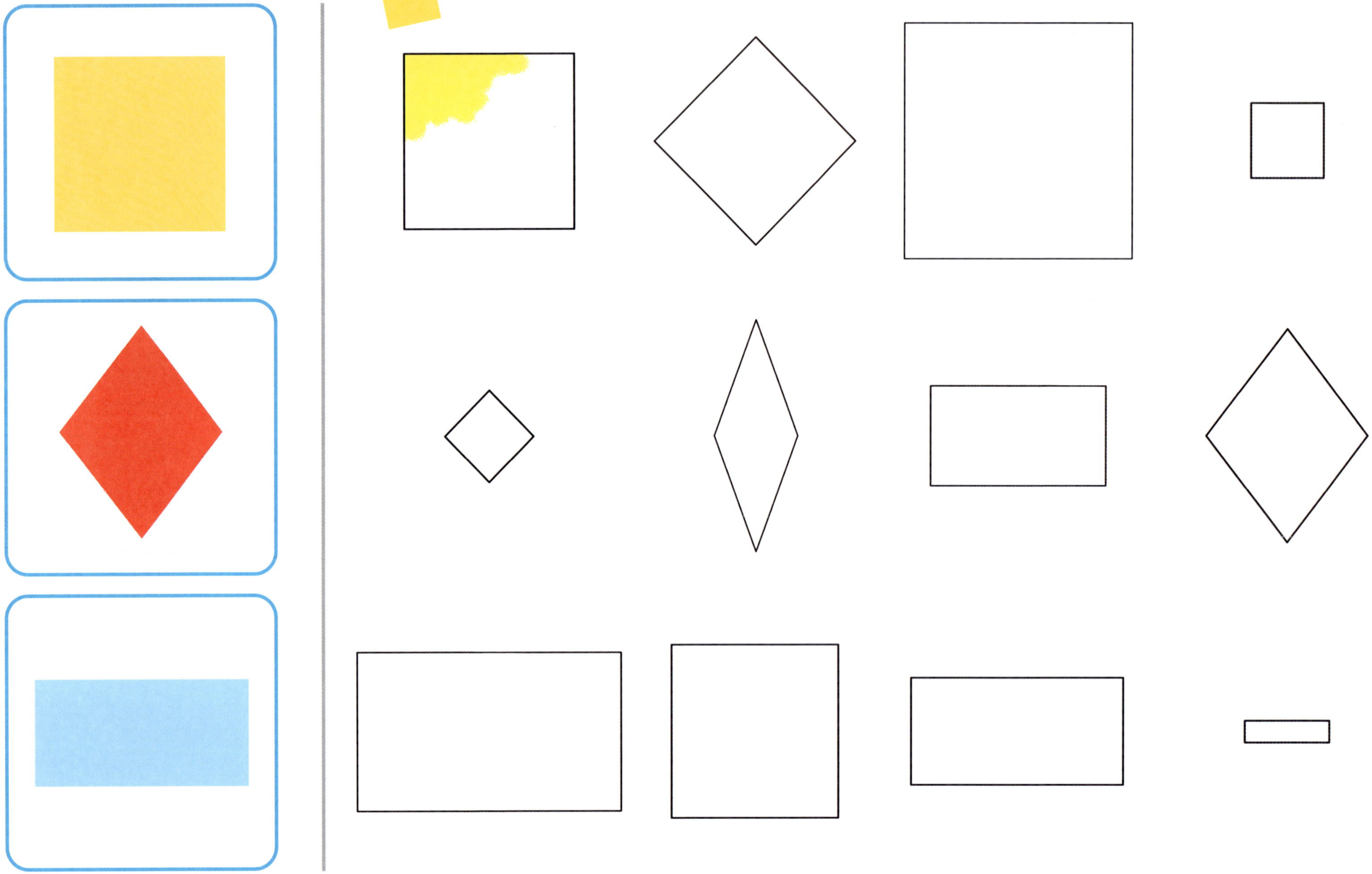

Find and color the shapes which are the same. Point and say.
Language: diamond, rectangle, square; colors

Concepts

Draw things for hot and cold weather. Point and say.
Language: hot, cold

Concepts

Color the frames of the pictures of noisy children red. Color the frames of the pictures of quiet children blue. Point and say. Language: noisy, quiet

Concepts

Match the objects to the correct places to clean up the classroom. Point and say.
Language: clean, messy

Festivals

Peace Day

Match. Color the things you love. Point and say.
Language: animals, bird, children, peace, world; I love the (bird).

Festivals

Carnival

Choose, draw and color your Carnival costume. Point and say.
Language: Carnival, clown, crown, king, pirate, queen; I'm a (pirate).

Festivals

Children's Day

Find and circle the children doing something different. Point and say.
Language: play, run, talk; I love to (talk).